S.W.A.G.

(Saved Woman Going After God)

Fashionable Devotions for Daily Life

Timethia,
Greatness resides within
you and is waiting to burst out!
Let God's light shine through
you that you might do His
will and fulfill
His purpose!

Krista Mincey

Love,
Kris

ISBN-13: 978-0-692-93059-5

Printed in the United States of America.

Published by Mincey Publishing

What People Are Saying about S.W.A.G. devotions…

This devotional gives young women a guide on how to navigate through life's many turns by knowing God and trusting in who He says they are. With practical advice grounded in the Word, this devotional is an honest and transparent view of the many difficulties young women deal with and gives them steps on how to work their way out.

Tia McCollors, Essence Bestselling Author, Speaker, and Writing Coach.

✢ ✢ ✢

S.W.A.G. is a thought-provoking devotional. Each day is written in such a real and relevant manner. I love the analogies with modern-day women's clothing and accessories.

Leading Lady Coylitia O'Neal, Global Impact Christian Ministries

✢ ✢ ✢

Who is God and what is grace? What happens when life gets messy? Why is a relationship with Jesus so important? And why does He care about me?

Young women are asking themselves these questions every day and God has an answer for them in S.W.A.G. I found this devotional to be a refreshing and unique in its approach to sharing the word of God. The author was able to pack a lot of thought and inspiration into each message.

Dr. Sherri Lewis, Physician, Essence Bestselling Author, Missionary, and Founder of Bethel Atlanta-Africa.

✛✛✛

S.W.A.G.'s devotions are uniquely tied to today's culture…

The message is clear! God loves us through all our lipstick and Spanx. Krista Mincey does a great job of stirring the heart of the reader with devotions grounded in spiritual truths, while being compared to everyday fashion and beauty items. The question of "Who I am in Christ?" is answered in a thoughtful and relatable way.

Rhonda McKnight, Award Winning Author, Speaker, and Founder of A Faith Worth Living Ministry.

Dedication

To that young girl who is unsure of herself and her place in life, trust in your journey and know that God works everything for your good.

To that young woman who is trying to find her way while dealing with the many bumps and turns that life takes us through, know that God sees you and is with you in every step.

To every woman who believes she is living the life God called her to live and wants to share her knowledge to the young women around her, continue to do your good work. You are how young women continue to grow into God.

Acknowledgements

I never imagined I would write the words that are on these pages. I never imagined that my life experiences would allow God to use me to convey a message of value, acceptance, and growth to young women. This devotional took many years, but it all worked in God's time.

I would like to thank Rhonda for guiding me through this process, having faith in this devotional, and pushing me to dig deep and pull out what was within me. To my mom and sister, thank you for your support through everything and helping me with edits. To my friends, thank you for your support and excitement for this project.

Table of Contents

Introduction

Becoming a woman comes with many challenges and missteps. Becoming a woman who is seeking to do God's will is even harder when you have doubts and are questioning things about:

- Yourself

- Who God really is

- What God's thoughts are towards you

As a young girl, I struggled to deal with the pain of my parent's divorce, my father leaving on my 8th birthday, and depression that lead to me attempting suicide. Throughout all my trails and challenges, one thing has always been consistent. When I truly understood who God was and who I was in Him, I viewed my circumstances differently and learned to accept and love myself more.

Looking back on my life, there are many instances when I needed someone to tell me things would be ok; that I wasn't the first person to go through this; and that I didn't need to be perfect for God to love me.

As a college professor, I am a firm believer that everyone wants to do better and be the best person they can be. I understand what stops many of us from achieving that goal is we never have anyone tell us how to get through the trials of life and how to learn to love ourselves and who God made us to be.

With this devotional, I hope to encourage you to grow deeper in God and understand that He thinks you are awesome and beautiful. I pray that as you read through these pages, you learn what steps to take to become the woman you were created to be. A woman full of promise whose current circumstances don't dictate where you will end up. I pray these devotionals cause you to have a better understanding of God and yourself.

If you are ready, I challenge you to go on this 30 day journey so that you can get your S.W.A.G. on!

Blessings,

Krista Mincey

1.

Spanx

In a society that is mainly focused on how a person looks, many women feel pressured to fit into the model of beauty displayed on magazine covers, music videos, Instagram, and Twitter. We believe that we aren't pretty enough or physically fit enough and have become obsessed with making our waists smaller and our butts bigger. We sometimes force ourselves into uncomfortable garments just so we can feel beautiful like the people we see on television. To that end, if you're like me, you probably own a few Spanx garments (stockings, control shorts, tops, pants, the list goes on) in different colors and sizes. If you don't own any now, you might consider purchasing one in the future. Spanx is a good product. Lord knows these things are miracle workers. They hide bumps; they hide lumps; they cloak cellulite; they even make your shape better, smoother, and smaller...Hallelujah!

When you step out with Spanx on, no one can tell you don't workout three times a week. They don't know you ate that delicious cake yesterday and all the rolls the restaurant brought to your table (guilty!). They don't know you have cellulite. They can't even tell where your real figure ends and the illusion of Spanx begins. The only way anyone would know your "flaws" is if you told them. Wearing Spanx makes you look your best and allows you to be your best without feeling your "flaws" are on display for everyone to see.

The same way Spanx covers all your flaws is the same way the blood of Jesus covers your sins. Our sins are the flaws of our soul, which are internal, not just a physical thing that will one day pass away. **When you put on the blood of Jesus, His blood covers all your sins no matter how old or new.** His blood smooths out everything in your life so no one can tell what you used to do or who you used to be when they look at you.

The disadvantage to Spanx is that it is a garment. A temporary solution to the bulges of life. When you take off the Spanx garment, you're back to the lumps and bumps you had before. When you put on the blood of Jesus, your transformation is PERMANENT! You won't have a reminder of what you used to be and people will never know who you used to be. Imagine if you were a prostitute. You'd probably think you would always be looked at as a prostitute and no one would be able to see the real you on the inside who wants to do more and have more. Because Jesus' blood covers all sin, this prostitute can have a transformation too. While it may seem strange for a prostitute to be transformed, this actually happened.

In Joshua 2, the Israelites were trying to step into the Promised Land that God gave them when they left slavery in Egypt. Like all good missions, Joshua sent people out to spy on the land in Jericho they were getting ready to take. When they arrived, they needed to hide from the soldiers so they went to the house of a prostitute named Rahab. While Rahab was a prostitute, she was familiar with the Israelite's story. She shared that she had heard about the Living God Israel served. A God who parted the Red Sea and gave the Israelites victory over their enemies. So, Rahab hid the men, asking one thing from them in return…that her family be spared when they returned to take the city. Now, Rahab's story could have ended here, but Jesus' blood did such a transformation that Rahab ended up being part of the direct blood line to the birth of baby Jesus. Only Jesus' blood can do a transformation like that. While people may know Rahab was a prostitute, that is not how she is remembered!

Just like Spanx, the only way anyone will know your past and all you did is if you tell them! When Jesus died on the cross, His blood paid for all your sins, wiped them clean, and gave you a new start. (Psalm 103:12) **If Jesus doesn't remember your wrongs, then why do you constantly remind yourself and tell others your past sins?** You're a new creature in Christ with Holy Ghost Spanx and it is time you embrace the new body your Spanx have given you instead of living in the past and reminding yourself who you used to be.

Scripture: 2 Corinthians 5:17

Affirmation: My past does not control my future.

Prayer:

Lord,

I thank you for dying for me on Calvary. I thank you for your blood washing away my sins. Lord, your word says my sins are as far as the east is from the west, so I pray Lord, that you wash me with your blood. I pray you clear my mind from my past and show me what you see when you look at me. Lord, let me move forward in the new life you've given me and not look back.

In Jesus' name, amen.

How to be Swaggalicious...

1. Read Romans 8:1-2. In the text it states, "There is no condemnation if you are in Christ," which means Jesus does not belittle you or remind you about what you did wrong. Why do we choose to keep reliving our past mistakes?

2. What wrongs are you constantly thinking about that are holding you back from stepping out and being the person you were called to be? Once you list these wrongs, pray about them, give them to God, and turn the page in your life. I recommend an exercise I use. Write the list of wrongs on a piece of paper and tear up the paper to show that you will not be bound by those wrongs anymore.

3. When you are getting dressed, look in the mirror and say "...I am fearfully and wonderfully made..." (Psalm 139:14). Keep saying this until you believe it so that you can truly leave your past in the past and step into true transformation.

_____

_____

_____

_____

_____

2.

Skinny Jeans

Skinny jeans are jeans made to basically look like a second skin because they fit so close to your body. Because they fit this way, you have to be confident in your shape and yourself to wear pants that don't hide anything. They are a fashion craze that exudes confidence. After all, you have to know that you can rock a jean that in and of itself means, "for thin people." On top of this, skinny jeans are usually hard to fit into because they are so…well…skinny.

I'll admit, when skinny jeans first came out, I was not a fan. I didn't understand why anyone would force themselves into pants that were skin tight. I just knew people couldn't be comfortably with jeans so fitted. After seeing so many people with them, I decided to squeeze myself into a pair. And squeeze I did.

I ended up getting my first pair of skinny jeans, one size smaller than I normally wear because my regular size was a little loose, and they didn't look bad. However, they were as tight as I imagined they would be. Since they were not the right size, I had to wear them with long shirts so I did not look like I was wearing jeans that were too small. After dealing with too small jeans, I finally bought a pair of skinny jeans in my actual size…my what a difference. I still had the fitted look without the sacrifice of my clothing being too tight!

The same way I was squeezing myself into jeans that were not my size is the same way **some of us try to squeeze ourselves into positions we are not supposed to be in because we want to be like so and so at school, church, or work**. When you see everyone around you in a certain job, with a certain car, and a certain life, you may think, "I want their life- or just a little of what they have." In reality, what you see people around you with may or may not be what they're supposed to have or be in. While you see it looking good on them, you don't know how much they may be struggling to look good in what they have.

Just like those skinny jeans come in different sizes, God's plan for us is custom fitted for each person. You may choose to squeeze into the plan God has for someone else like I squeezed into those too small skinny jeans. Or you can put on the plan God customized especially for you and not have to work hard to try and fit into someone else's plan.

One of the Ten Commandments that God gave Moses in Exodus Chapter 20 says that we should not covet anything our neighbor has. This simply means that we should not desire the things that those around us have. This doesn't mean that you can't use other people as motivation to achieve things. It means that you shouldn't want their things.

Imagine you're in the grocery store and your cart is filled with all the items you needed to purchase. All of a sudden, someone comes along and takes your cart with all your items. You ask, "Why didn't you get your own cart and shop instead of taking mine?" They reply, "I liked what you had in your cart and wanted your things instead of having to work to get them." This is an example of coveting what your neighbor has.

Like my new skinny jeans give me the same look without discomfort, choosing God's custom plan for you gives you the same blessing He has for you without all the stress and extra work of wanting exactly what someone else has without knowing what they had to do to have what you see them with. What God designs for you is for you and only you can walk in those skinny jeans and make it look so easy!

Scripture: Exodus 20:17

Affirmation: God has given me all I need.

Prayer:

Dear Lord,

I thank you for making me who I am. I thank you that what you have for me is for me and no one else. Lord, I pray you take away my desire to have what others have and replace that desire with the things you want me to have.

In Jesus' name, amen.

How to be Swaggalicious...

1. What things do you see others with that you wish were yours?

2. What things in your life are you happy about being

things that only you have? For example, are you happy that you're an only child or that you have great fashion sense?

3. What steps can you take to work toward the things that you want to do in your life?

_____

_____

_____

_____

_____

_____

_____

_____

_____

_____

_____

_____

_____

_____

_____

_____

_____

_____

_____

_____

_____

_____

_____

_____

_____

3.

Watch

With everyone having a cell phone now, a watch's purpose has moved from telling time to showing a sense of style and fashion. There are designer watches, watches in every color, watches with different bands, watches with stones or diamonds. Watches are so different, you could have one to match every outfit or whatever your mood is for the day.

Since a watch can be for function or fashion, a lot of people feel naked if they leave the house without one. My mother is like that. I know she has a watch for every outfit. I, on the other hand, have never been a big watch person. I think they're nice, but I don't have to wear one every day. My thinking is, I have my cell phone which has a clock so I can just check it if I need to know the time.

When I do wear a watch, I notice that I'm always checking my wrist to see what time it is! If I'm in class and ready to go, I look at my watch to start counting down how much time is left. If I'm in a meeting, I'm checking it to see how long I've been in there. If I'm waiting on important information, I'm constantly checking my watch to see if I'll get the information before the end of the day. Like I am constantly checking my physical watch to see how long I've been somewhere or how much longer I had to wait for food, we sometimes check our spiritual watch constantly to see how long we've been waiting for God to do something.

Just like looking at your physical watch doesn't make your time at work move any faster, looking at your spiritual watch and constantly reminding God how long you've been waiting for something doesn't make Him move faster either. **We are so busy trying to get to the next thing, the next day that we fail to enjoy the season we're in or explore the lessons God wants us to learn in the present.**

Yes, God wants you to have that brand new car, but maybe the reason you haven't gotten it yet is because He wants you to learn to appreciate the things you have now so that when He gives you the car, you take care of it. Yes, God wants you to have the boo of your dreams, but maybe He wants you to find your purpose in Him before He gives you your desires.

God's time is not our time. I repeat GOD'S TIME IS NOT OUR TIME! In His world, time does not exist. While you may think you should have already gotten what you're praying for, God knows the perfect time to bring you what you want. Chapter 3 of Ecclesiastes talks about there being a time for everything. It goes on further to say that God makes everything appropriate in His time, meaning that when you're ready for whatever you're praying for, He will send it to you. Just because there's been a delay in your prayer request, doesn't mean God has denied your request or forgotten about it.

Instead of looking at your spiritual watch counting the minutes, hours, days, and months it's taking for your prayers to come to pass, take time to learn what lessons God wants to teach you during your time of waiting.

Scripture: Ecclesiastes 3:1

Affirmation: God is bringing me what is mine in His time.

Prayer:

Dear Lord,

I thank you for what You have done for me and the blessings You've given me. I thank You for bringing me my desires in your perfect time. Lord, I pray you strengthen me as I wait and that you give me a spirit of peace and calmness knowing You are concerned about my affairs.

In Jesus' name, amen.

How to be Swaggalicious...

1. What have you been praying for that you feel God hasn't provided yet?

2. Why do you think God hasn't answered your prayer(s)?

3. What things can you do while you wait for God to answer your prayer(s)?

_____

_____

_____

_____

_____

4.

Sneakers

From exercise, dancing, or leisure, you can find a sneaker to fit any activity you are looking to do. With the many color options and styles, sneakers have almost become like high heels, with many people having multiple pairs of sneakers to go with different outfits. Even though I like heels and think they make me feel extra feminine and pretty, nothing beats my sneakers! My sneakers give support and allow me to walk or run without my feet hurting. Most importantly, my sneakers signal to me…comfort. If you've ever noticed people in sneakers, they always walk like they're comfortable because their feet don't hurt so they're able to walk longer or stand longer. When I'm in my sneakers, I'm able to remove the outward things like fancy clothes and shoes that impress others and get back to the real me.

Our Christian walk is that way, too. We dress up the outside by memorizing key scriptures, talking the way we think Christians are supposed to talk, and saying prayers that we think we're supposed to pray. While these acts may gain the attention and admiration of others, they do not faze God. God simply wants us to be real and honest with Him. He wants us to take off the high heels, pretty dresses, and churchy ways so that He can work on the real us. God wants us to be so comfortable in Him and our relationship with Him that we are not concerned about trying to look a certain way so the world knows how deep our walk with God is. He knows that if we are honest and real with Him, people will be able to see our relationship with Him.

In Matthew Chapter 5, verse 16, it tells us to let our light shine so that others will glorify God. **If you allow yourself to be vulnerable and open in your relationship with God, He will grow and develop you into the woman He destined you to be.** As you grow in your relationship with Him, your change will be noticeable by all. They will be able to see that you talk different, walk different, and have a different demeanor about yourself. When they start asking you what's different about you, you'll say…God and He will get the glory and you may even draw them to God because they see a change in you.

So the next time you put on your heels, remember to keep your sneakers close by when you need a reminder to remain real and authentic in your walk with God.

Scripture: Matthew 5: 14-16

Affirmation: God loves me for me and wants His light to shine through me.

Prayer:

Lord,

I thank you for knowing the real me and still loving me. Lord, I pray that you keep me authentic in my walk with

You and that You allow me to be a reflection of You and Your word. Lord, I pray that You remove any action I do to please others and not You. I pray that You renew my mind and keep me focused on my relationship with You.

In Jesus' name, amen.

How to be Swaggalicious...

1. What do you like about your physical appearance?

2. What do you think people see when they look at you? Is there evidence to support your thought?

3. What can you do to be more comfortable with who you are as a person?

_____
_____
_____
_____
_____
_____
_____
_____
_____
_____
_____
_____
_____
_____
_____
_____
_____
_____
_____

5.

Peep-toe

A nice pair of peep-toe shoes is a boss fashionable addition to any woman's shoe collection and a must-have wardrobe item in the summer. And in-between manicures, a peep-toe shoe can hide your truth, because you only have to worry about making sure the toes that show are painted! Come on, you know that's why you wear them.

Even though these are great reasons to own a pair of peep-toe shoes, they just aren't for me. I have tried many times to wear peep-toe shoes, but you can never see my short and stubby toes through the peep part, so I don't bother. While a peep-toe doesn't show anything for me, some like that a peep-toe only allows people to see a little, not everything. Many Christians are the same way; they only want to show others their peep-toe.

We want everyone to know how well we can pray and how many Scriptures we can recite. What we don't want them to see is what's hiding under the shoe; our unforgiveness, addiction, depression, insecurity, overeating, unfaithfulness, and all the other things we can't "dress up".

Have you ever noticed that people who wear peep-toes, never take their shoes off around people?

Even if their feet hurt, they can't take their shoes off for fear someone will see what is hiding underneath. Not dealing with their issues, has essentially held them hostage to their peep-toe shoe and the pain that may come from the shoe.

The same can happen in our spiritual life. **If we don't deal with our "issues" of unforgiveness, addiction, anger, selfishness, and jealousy; then they hold us captive.** We are unable to move in the things of God because we're afraid of our "issues" getting out. Since we haven't dealt with them, God can't use us to our full potential because our "issues" will always come up and will always hinder us from moving forward.

So remember to always work on your issues and not just reveal the ones that show through your peep-toe. By dealing with our "issues" we are able to show all of God that is working in us and we're able to move freely and walk into the things of God.

Scripture: 2 Corinthians 5:17

Affirmation: My [name your issue] does not define me and will not hold me back from becoming who God created me to be.

Prayer:

Lord,

Forgive me for trying to cover up the things that You want to help me deal with. I realize that I can't fix my issues on my own, and I need Your help. I pray that You remove what is not like You and develop me into whom You have called me to be. Lord, show me what I need to do so that I can be more like You.

In Jesus' name, amen.

How to be Swaggalicious…

1. What issues are you hiding from other people?

2. How have you tried to work on these issues?

3. What steps can you take to address one of the issues you mentioned?

_____

_____

_____

_____

_____

_____

_____

_____

_____

_____

_____

_____

_____

_____

_____

_____

_____

_____

_____

_____

_____

_____

6.

Mirror

Mirrors are almost everywhere. They're in your car, in your bathroom, and in dressing rooms at the mall. Regardless of where a mirror is located, it serves the same purpose. A mirror's purpose is to help you see. The mirror in your car helps you see what is behind you and on the side of you so that you don't have a car accident. Mirrors in a bathroom or a dressing room help you see how you look so you don't walk out with your hair undone or buy clothes that you don't like.

As women, most of us carry a mirror at all times so we know how we look when we're meeting people. A mirror allows us to see a reflection of ourselves and view what others see when they look at us. Not only does a mirror allow you to see yourself the way others see you, it also allows you to see yourself for what you really look like--good and bad. Maybe viewing yourself in the mirror has allowed you to embrace your curves or has encouraged you to start going to the gym. Maybe the mirror allows you to see how beautiful you are, despite your flaws and imperfections.

Not only do mirrors allow us to see the good, they also allow us to see the bad. When you use a magnifying mirror, you're able to see every imperfection on your face that was "hiding" from your view in the regular mirror. Our spiritual mirror, the Holy Spirit, is the same way. In John Chapter 14, verse 26 Jesus tells His disciples that while He is leaving, He is leaving them with a Helper, the Holy Spirit, who will teach them all things. The Holy Spirit allows us to see our beauty and to accept our flaws. As we dig deeper, He reveals the areas we need to remove, work on, or enhance so that we are a reflection of God. Just like you have to use a magnifying mirror to see what is hiding, you have to allow the Holy Spirit to come in and reveal where you need improvement.

When God created you, you were created in His image (Genesis 1:27). **Since you are created in His image, you should reflect things that mirror Him**. You should show love and compassion to your enemies and friends. You should see beyond someone's flaws or shortcomings. The reason you should do these things is because this is how Jesus is with us. He shows us love and compassion despite all we do, and He looks beyond our "issues" and flaws to see the person we are. If the same God who created us can do those things, then as His creation, we can do the same.

In order to reflect God, we have to know God and know the things of Him. The only way to know God is through quiet time with Him in prayer and in reading His Word. His Word reveals who He is. When we know who He is, we know what we should strive to become. Because prayer is simply a conversation with God, the more we do it, the more we get closer to Him and learn about Him.

Mirrors only reflect what's in front of them. If you don't have Christ-like qualities in you, then your mirror won't reflect that. Even if you do reflect Christ, all mirrors need to be cleaned so they continue to clearly reflect the image in front of them. So when you look at your reflection in the mirror, make sure you not only see the physical you, but Christ who is being reflected in you.

Scripture: Genesis 1:27

Affirmation: I reflect Christ in all that I do.

Prayer:

Dear God,

I thank You for sending the Holy Spirit to help me work on the things I need to address. I pray that You remove what is not like You and replace it with the things of you so that I may be a reflection of You. I make myself fully available to You and ask that You have Your way in my life.

In Jesus' name, amen.

How to be Swaggalicious...

1. What spiritual flaws do you need to work on?

2. How do you develop a better relationship with God?

3. What things can you do on a daily basis to be more like God?

_____

_____

_____

_____

7.

Workout

When most hear the phrase "work-out" they either love it, tolerate it, or hate it. Let's be honest, most people don't like working out. Working out regularly is a habit that you have to develop over time for it to become part of your life. When I was in high school, I tolerated gym class because it was something we were required to take. When I was in my early twenties, my dad had a heart attack, and I had a diabetes scare, so I started taking my health more seriously and started working out. Now that I am in my thirties, I enjoy working out because I know it's good for my health, makes me feel good, and makes me look good.

Growing in God is the same way. In First Corinthians, Chapter 13, verse 11 the Bible talks about growth and that when you are a child, you do child like things but when you grow up, you don't do things that a child would do. When you were young, you may have gone to church because your parents, grandparents, or someone made you go. When you got older (teenage or young adult), you may have still been going to church out of habit or because someone was making you go, but you may have also been involved with different activities or ministries at church that may have made going to church more enjoyable. When you reach adulthood, you may have gone through some things (death of a loved one, unemployment, difficulty in school) and realized how important your relationship with God is. While you still may go to church out of a routine or habit, the things you have gone through compel you to want more when you go to church. You want to go to church to get a Word, and you want to go so that you can grow in the things of God.

That is growing in God! Just like you have to go through sacrifice and pain, and have a desire to exercise to grow physically; spiritual growth requires you to do the same thing! **Loving and wanting to spend time with God isn't something that's automatic. It's something we have to work at and discipline ourselves to do until it becomes a habit and behavior that is natural and we can't imagine not doing!**

No one starts out loving to work out and wanting to do it every day. You start small and as you gain momentum, you increase your workout time, exercise, and the number of days and the length of conditions. You even begin to vary the types of exercise and workouts that you do from weight training to cardio, to water aerobics.

Spiritual growth is no different. Start small with a devotional and short prayer. As you do that consistently and build momentum, delve more into the Word and increase your prayer time. As you do these things, you will begin to grow and won't be able to imagine not spending time with God on a daily basis.

Scripture: 1 Corinthians 13: 11

Affirmation: I am growing in the things of God daily.

Prayer:

Dear Lord,

Thank You for bringing me this far. I pray that You continue to grow and develop me into the woman You have destined me to be. Let Your desires become my desires so that I can grow in the things of You. Draw me closer to You each day so that time with You won't become routine or duty but a desire.

In Jesus' name, amen.

How to be Swaggalicious...

1. What things did you do as a child that you no longer do anymore?

2. What things did you do as a child that you still do?

3. In what ways can you stop doing the childish things that you continue to do? If you aren't doing childish things, in what ways can you do more things that a woman should do?

_____

_____

_____

_____

_____

_____

_____

_____

_____

8.

Bright Nails

I admit to not being that girly of a girl. Certainly not the kind that wanted to repaint my nails often, so I never used to like getting my finger nails painted with colored nail polish. I knew they were going to chip and everyone would be able to tell that I needed a fresh coat of polish. When I did paint my nails, I only used pale colors or a clear polish. However, lately, I've started painting my nails more and don't want to use pale colors. I actually prefer using colors that stand out! I've decided if I'm going to paint them, why not choose a color that will stand out.

Many of us are pale Christians who don't stand out. We blend in like my pale nail polish. You believe in God and have a true relationship with Him, but no one knows about your walk with God because you don't say anything or stand out as a Christian. Matthew Chapter 5, verse 14 says that we are the light of the word. Think about that, if we are the light of the world, then we have to shine brightly so that no parts of the world are in darkness. **When the sun doesn't shine, we have cloudy, dark days. When we don't shine the light God has given us, the world has cloudy, dark days, too.**

You may shy away from being bold because you

think you aren't good enough or you're too messed up for anyone to listen to you or for God to use you. The Bible has numerous stories of God using the most unlikely person to deliver His message and change the world. He used Moses to lead the children of Israel out of slavery (Exodus). He used Rahab to save the spies (Joshua 2). He used Esther to save the Jews (Esther). And He used a virgin to give birth to His son, Jesus, who came to save the world (Matthew 27). Throughout history, God always uses the least likely to reach the masses (1 Corinthians 1:27).

If you proclaim to be a Christian, it's time to be bold in your walk and stand out among the crowd. Some people may never read the Bible or go to church, but seeing you choosing to live boldly for Christ could draw them to God. Imagine how many people would turn to God and change their life if we Christians stopped being pale and started being bold in Christ and letting His light shine through us. Jesus said He is the light of the world (John 8: 12). Since we are made in His image, we are to be the light, too.

Today, put away your pale Christianity and replace it with boldness that lets your light shine!

Scripture: Matthew 5:14, John 8:12

Affirmation: I will let God shine His light through me.

Prayer:

Dear Lord,

I thank You for boldness today. Lord, I pray You let Your light shine through me so that it draws people unto

You. I pray You give me boldness to speak Your word and to live a life that is pleasing unto You.

In Jesus' name amen.

How to be Swaggalicious...

1. What makes you scared to let others know about your walk with Christ?

2. What would make you more comfortable with living your life boldly for Christ?

3. What steps can you take to start living a bold Christian life that impacts those around you?

_____

_____

_____

_____

_____

_____

_____

_____

_____

_____

_____

_____

_____

_____

_____

_____

_____

_____

_____

9.

Little Black Dress

A black dress is a wardrobe item that stylists say all women should have in their closet. A black dress is an item of clothing that works for any event (graduation, date, job interview, or church). A black dress can be dressed up with a dressy heels and a nice necklace or dressed down with flats and a jean jacket. While the type of black dress you have may change over the years due to weight or style changes, the black dress's ability to fit with any occasion or environment doesn't change. Although you have other dresses or outfits in your closet, you always keep your little black dress handy and ready to go when you need it.

The Word of God is the same way. You keep it within you so that you can pull it out when you face difficult times and need a word to fit your situation that will make you feel good. While you may outgrow your little black dress, you will never outgrow God's word. Having God's word available for every occasion requires you to do a little work.

Psalms 119, verse 11 talks about hiding the Word of God in your heart. This doesn't literally mean hide the Word in your heart, but it's talking about having the Word in your spirit so that when you need it, you have it with you. Imagine you're out somewhere and lose your cell phone. You're by yourself and need to call someone to come and pick you up. Someone lets you borrow their phone to call someone, but you don't know what number to dial because all your numbers are in your phone and you don't know any of them by heart. The numbers do you no good if they are only in the phone you don't have access to. The same can be said for the Word of God. **If you don't know any Word** (one Scripture or more Scriptures) **and have to have a Bible near you to get it, then it does you no good when you're in a place where you need the Word**--like a bad relationship, problems with school, or problems with parents.

When difficult times hit, we always go back to what we know first. This is why you always go for your little, black dress because it's what you know. So the next time you pull out your little black dress, make sure your spiritual, little, black dress is ready to go, too!

Scripture: Psalms 119:11

Affirmation: I carry God's Word with me every day.

Prayer:

Lord,

I ask You to strengthen me daily in Your Word that it may rest on my heart. Lord, give me the passion I need to take in Your word so I can call on it in my time of need.

In Jesus' name, amen.

How to be Swaggalicious...

1. How do you handle difficult times (a bad grade, fight with a parent, fight with a friend)?

2. How could you handle these situations better?

3. What steps can you take so that you can carry God's Word in your spirit daily?

_____

_____

_____

_____

_____

_____

_____

_____

_____

_____

_____

_____

_____

_____

_____

_____

_____

_____

_____

_____

_____

_____

_____

10.

Stilettos

Stilettos are high heel shoes with very skinny heels. Stilettos are usually a little uncomfortable to wear because they are high and the skinny heel means you have very little to walk on. Despite all of this, many women wear stilettos on a regular basis without any problem. Like anything, the key to stilettos is learning how to walk in them.

I didn't want to give in to wearing stilettos, but the shoes were so stylish and looked good on my feet. Dealing with a little pain to look good didn't seem like a bad trade off to me. As I got older, I started to care less about fashion and more about comfort. Although I don't wear super high heels anymore, I still love the way they look.

Walking in stilettos requires skill, patience, and grace so you don't fall flat on your face. You have to know what you're doing to wear stilettos. You can view walking with God the same way. When you put on stilettos, you automatically know that walking in them isn't going to be easy. **Walking with God requires you to be determined to follow after Him and do His will and have patience to remain with Him when the trials of life come at you.**

In Luke, Chapter 9, Jesus is talking to His disciples

(12 main followers) about how difficult their journey with Him is going to be. He tells them that following Him means they have to give up their life as they know it. While this is a difficult thing for anyone to do, Jesus comforts the disciples by telling them that if they give up their life and their way for Him, they will save their life, while those who want to keep their own way will lose their life. Jesus isn't saying they will face a physical death by not giving up their ways to follow Him. Jesus is saying they will face a spiritual death. Choosing to do things your way without God means that you are separated from Him and don't have relationship. In order to be alive spiritually, you have to have relationship with God.

Walking in stilettos may cause you to fall and face embarrassment from those around you. When you walk with God, His grace covers you when you fall and protects you from the embarrassment and ridicule of others. While God is protecting you with His grace, He gives you the skill to know how to walk with Him as you move forward in life. Someone who has just started wearing stilettos has shaky, unsure steps. Someone who has mastered stilettos walks in them like they're sneakers.

New Christians are shaky in their walk with God while they figure everything out and learn more about God. After you learn more about God and go through trials that increase your faith, your walk is straighter and you make Christianity look so simple to everyone around you. If your spiritual stilettos are a little shaky, trust that God's grace will give you the skill and the patience to walk like a supermodel!

Scripture: Luke 9: 21-27

Affirmation: I am walking better in the things of God daily.

Prayer:

Dear Lord,

I ask for Your grace to be with me as I walk in Your will. Lord, I know that You are strong where I am weak, and I need Your strength to make it through. I pray You give me the skills I need to be more like You and that You change anything in me that would hinder my walk with You.

In Jesus' name, amen.

How to be Swaggalicious...

1. What things (prayer, reading Bible, a certain sin) are you struggling to do with your Christian walk?

2. Why do you think doing these things is difficult for you?

3. Who can you talk to that can help you with these things?

_____

_____

_____

_____

_____

_____

_____

11.

Capris

Capris are pants that fall between your knee and ankle. They're too long to be considered shorts, but not long enough to be considered pants. Because I'm short, Capri's always make me look like I'm wearing pants that are too short. I'm not able to carry off the Capri effect, and for this reason, I don't like Capri's. When I wear Capri's, I don't want there to be any doubt about the fashion statement I'm trying to make.

As Christians, some of us are like me in Capri pants. People can't tell if you're knee deep or all the way in! Sometimes our actions don't match our words and because of this, people doubt your relationship with God. When people see you, they should be able to tell that you're sold out for God, and not have doubt about you being a follower of Christ.

James Chapter 1, verse 6 says that a person who doubts is like waves in the sea because they move back and forth. It goes on to say this type of person won't get anything from God and they are unstable. Think about the brakes on your car. When you're driving, you don't want to have any doubts that your brakes will work when you use them to make your car stop. If you were unsure of the brakes in your car, you might not drive the car because you wouldn't be sure the car would stop when you needed it to stop.

If you are a wavering Christian, it is hard for God to use you. If one day you're with God, and the next day you don't want to do things God's way, you are not a person He can have faith in to use for His will. For many people you encounter, you're the only "Bible" they will see or read. It would be sad if someone didn't come to God because they couldn't believe in what they see in you, because your actions gave them doubts that you were truly living for Christ.

Your relationship with God is like any other relationship--either you're fully in or you're not. Even though God still loves us and His grace is sufficient in our weakness and sin, He knows we won't get His full benefits until we're completely sold out to Him. If you were dating a guy and he always told you he loved you, but his actions said he could care less, you probably wouldn't stay around because his actions don't match his words.

If you are looking for your significant other's actions to match their words, how much more do you think God wants your profession of being a Christian to match your actions? When you step out today, make sure wherever you are in your walk with God, that you are fully committed to it and that your actions match your words. Make sure people know how deep your spiritual pants go.

Scripture: James 1: 6-8

Affirmation: I am sold out for God and He is reflected in all that I do.

Prayer:

Dear Lord, I thank You for loving me in spite of all my wrongs. I ask You to cleanse me of anything that does not reflect You. Lord, I want people to be drawn to You through my actions. Lord, I ask You to work on me so I can be sold out for You.

In Jesus' name, amen.

How to be Swaggalicious...

1. What characteristics do others use to describe you? List attributes that are positive and negative.

2. Do these characteristics reflect characteristics that Jesus' displays? (forgiving, loving, non-judgmental)

3. Which characteristic from number 1 would you like to change? List ways that you can work on changing this characteristic to reflect the character of Jesus.

_____

_____

_____

_____

_____

_____

_____

_____

_____

_____

_____

_____

_____

_____

_____

_____

_____

_____

_____

_____

_____

_____

_____

12.

Diamonds

Diamonds are said to be a girl's best friend. They are an expensive gem that has to go through a process to become the shiny stones that many of us love. There's something about the way a diamond shines that makes you stop and look at it and the person who is wearing it. I have one pair of real diamond earrings that I received as a Christmas gift from my dad when I was five years old. As I have gotten older, I tend to wear my diamond earrings more because I realize that diamonds are supposed to be seen, not hidden. Whether you already own some, don't have any, or you're rockin' fake ones, diamonds are something that should always be shown off and never hidden.

While we admire the beauty of a polished diamond, we rarely admire the potential beauty of the carbon that diamonds come from. Most of us are only interested in the finished product that is the diamond, not the process the carbon went through. For a diamond to form, the coal must be in darkness and have pressure applied to it.

When you allow God to mold and press you through trials, you, too, become like that carbon. After being in dark situations such as unemployment, illness, loss of a loved one, or struggles in school or relationships,

God uses the darkness and pressure of trials to take you from carbon and **make you into the diamond He knew you could always be!**

James, Chapter 1, verse 2 says that we should rejoice when we face trials. Rejoicing when your parent or loved one dies, you're facing an unexpected illness, or you're dealing with personal struggles doesn't seem logical. Why rejoice when you're sad, crying, and in despair? James tells us that we rejoice because trails test our faith and this testing produces perseverance and perseverance helps you grow and develop. Think about the last hard thing you went through. After you made it through that trial, you probably felt like you had grown as a person and become more mature and could handle more difficult things. This is why we rejoice when trials come. We spiritually mature in the process. Just like coal can't become a diamond without darkness and pressure, you can't become who God called you to be without trails that test you and make you grow.

Once a diamond has been formed, it remains that way and doesn't go back to what it was (coal) when it was in darkness. Diamonds shine whether in the dark or the light (Matthew 5:14). If diamonds always shine, you can do the same. Once you come out of the dark, don't let difficult situations pull you back into the dark by taking your zest for life or God away. You're God's diamond.

Scripture: James 1:2-4

Affirmation: My trials make me shine brighter for

God.

Prayer:

Dear Lord, thank You for the trials You have brought me through and are taking me through right now. I know they will only make me into the woman of God You have called me to be. Lord I pray You keep me strong while I'm in the dark so that I can shine and radiate Your life.

In Jesus' name, amen.

How to be Swaggalicious...

1. What difficult things have you dealt with in the past or are you dealing with right now?

2. How have these difficult trials changed you (good or bad)?

3. What did you learn going through these trials?

_____

_____

_____

_____

_____

_____

_____

_____

_____

_____

_____

_____

_____

13.

Designer Bag

Purses and bags these days are more about style and less about function. Some people only carry name brand bags. Some make sure to match their bag to their outfit, while others carry whatever looks good and is affordable. I never really liked purses growing up. I didn't see the need to carry one when I had pockets and a book bag that could hold what I needed. When I did start carrying a purse, I liked a certain brand and faithfully purchased it. I didn't think much about the inside of the purse or even if it would be functional. I just wanted it to look good. As I've gotten older, I have expanded the type of bag that I like, but I still buy purses based on how they look on the outside, not if they are functional on the inside.

Many of us are the same way with our walk with God. We're more concerned with how we look on the outside instead of paying more attention to what is on the inside. We make sure we're dressed to the nines, and our hair and makeup are just right, but if the truth were told, many of us are putting on a show.

1 Peter, Chapter 3, verse 3 says that you shouldn't only be focused on your outer appearance, but you should focus on your inner man (woman) because that is what is great in God's eyes. This doesn't mean

that God doesn't want you to look nice. This means that God wants you to make sure that the inner you matches the outer you. Proverbs 31:30 says "Charm is deceptive, and beauty fleeting…" Think about the most beautiful woman you know. Does she also have a beautiful spirit? Is she kind, helpful, and friendly? Most people who are beautiful on the inside, reflect that beauty on the outside. However, people who are mean, hurtful, and rude will make their outside appear to be not so beautiful, even it actually is.

God sees you all dressed up and going to church, but He's checking on the inside to see how authentic your heart is (1 Samuel 16:7). When God sent Samuel to Jesse's house to anoint the next king, Samuel focused on the outer appearance of Jesse's sons and assumed they were the chosen one because of how they looked. But God didn't look at their outer appearance, He looked at their heart. God rejected all of Jesse's sons except David, who was said to be a man after God's own heart, and became the King of Israel.

God doesn't care how you dress yourself up for people on Sunday morning or Wednesday Bible study. **God wants to know if the outer man you display is the same man you show Him!** God is always more concerned about what's on the inside than what's on the outside. God wants the outside of your designer bag to match the inside. He wants the real thing!

Scripture: 1 Samuel 16: 7

Affirmation: I am becoming the woman God wants me to be from the inside out.

Prayer:

Dear Lord, I repent for not being as authentic as You want me to be. I ask You to search my heart and remove what is not like You. Lord, let my relationship with You be authentic and pleasing to You.

In Jesus' name, amen.

How to be Swaggalicious...

1. Do you think people judge you based on your outer appearance? Why or why not? Do you find yourself judging people based on their appearance?

2. How does being judged by your appearance affect you?

3. What steps can you take to focus on the appearance of your "inner" woman?

_____

_____

_____

_____

_____

_____

_____

_____

_____

_____

_____

_____

_____

_____

_____

14.

Identification

Identification is usually a document that shows and verifies to others who you are. Examples are your driver's license, school ID, and passport. Identification also allows you access to certain places and allows you to do certain things. While all these forms of identification allow you to do certain things, they also come with rules and responsibilities.

When I got my driver's license, I was so excited to show people my picture and to be able to drive. I felt the same way about my college ID too. I wanted to show everyone I was in college. In the beginning, it was never an inconvenience for me to have to pull out my college ID, I was glad I had it. After the newness of showing my ID wore off and the reality of having it kicked in, my excitement wore off. Having a license meant I was now running errands and had to think about money for gas and car repairs. A college ID meant I was taking five or six classes and working long hours to pass them.

Christianity is the same way. While you may love flashing your "ID" and letting everyone know you're a Christian, having that "ID" comes with work and responsibility. If you say you're a Christian, you have to spend time with God, time reading His word, time meditating on His word, time in prayer, and time in worship.

In Matthew, Chapter 16, verse 24 Jesus tells the disciples that to follow Him, they have to take up their cross. It's the same for us. This doesn't mean we must carry a physical cross. It means that we must be willing to do the things that Jesus did with the ultimate dying on the cross. This verse shows that being a follower of Christ is not easy and will require some sacrifice.

Even though my license and college ID came with responsibility, having them came with perks too! Having a license meant I could vote, open bank accounts, and fly on a plane. My college ID gave me access to discounts, events, and games. Having a relationship with God comes with benefits as well. While walking with Him requires work, it has a lot of perks. You have access to grace and mercy for free. You have access to His blessings and you have eternal life (John 3:16).

Yes, **carrying your God "ID" means work, but it also means access to a life above and beyond your dreams!** So before you leave the house, make sure you have your "ID" on you in case you need access to restricted areas.

Scripture: Matthew 16:24-25

Affirmation: My identity in Christ gives me access and the ability to do all that I want to do.

Prayer:

Lord, I thank You for Your presence in my life. I thank

You for being able to be called a follower of You. I pray You give me strength to make it through the work of being a Christian knowing Your reward is at the end.

In Jesus' name, amen.

How to be Swaggalicious...

1. What words would you use to identify yourself? (woman, short, tall, etc.)

2. How do these words impact who you are?

3. Think about your walk with Christ. How do you think being a follower impacts your identity and your life in a negative way?

  a. Now think about how being a follower of Christ impacts your identity and life in a positive way.

_____

_____

_____

_____

_____

_____

_____

_____

_____

_____

_____

_____

_____

_____

_____

15.

Hairpins

Hairpins are an accessory a woman uses to pull her hair back or to keep it in a certain style. They come curved, long, short, with gems, or in different colors. Regardless of what hairpins look like, their function remains the same, to keep hair in place. Because hair can get unruly or out of place at any time, it helps to have hairpins on you at all times.

Have you ever had your outfit together and were ready to step out, only to realize your hair is everywhere and not so put together? Instead of people focusing on everything you have right, they're going to focus on the thing that isn't so right. Most will wonder, how could she step out dressed so nicely and not take the time to fix her hair.

Now sometimes you may just be in a rush and not have time to get everything presentable, or you leave your house believing things are right until someone lets you know that something is out of place. When problems like this arise, it's always helpful to have a few hairpins on hand that will help you get your hair in order. Having access to hairpins gives you the opportunity to get things right, no matter the situation or circumstances.

The same way hairpins bring order to your hairdo;

spiritual hairpins keep you together as you go through trials and life circumstances. Sometimes life can throw you so many curve balls and take you on so many twists and turns that you can't make sense of anything. But God's Word tells us we are not alone and we are not without help. **When you use hairpins like praise, prayer, fasting, and meditation, you're able to get yourself together so you can do what you need to do to move forward.**

In Philippians, Chapter 4, verse 6, it says to not be anxious about anything. This means that we should never be nervous or worried about any situation we face or go through. This may seem hard to do if you're facing a really big obstacle, or you're concerned about certain things in your life working out, but it doesn't matter. Whatever the situation, we should not be anxious about it.

The Word tells us in verse 6 that we are to make our request known to God through prayer, petition, and thanksgiving. This means that instead of worrying, we need to pray and petition God for the thing we need Him to work out. Not only do we pray to God, we also thank God. Psalms 100:4 says we should enter His gates with thanksgiving and His courts with praise. It doesn't say only when things are going right. It just says we should do it, which means we praise and give God thanksgiving at all times. Doing these things is how we learn to not be anxious and to trust God to bring everything together.

Even though hairpins are good, you have to use them to get the benefit. You also have to always have them with you in case an emergency occurs and you need them. You can't only pray in church or just in the morning or night. You must pray constantly without ceasing whenever you feel things in your life are out of order. Some may carry the Word or prayer, but if you never call on the Word in meditation or press God on His word through prayer, then these hairpins are no good to you because you aren't using them. Carrying and using your spiritual hairpins enables you to pull yourself together whatever the situation, and to be who God called you to be.

Scripture: Philippians 4:6-7

Affirmation: As I pray and trust God, He holds me together in all that I go through.

Prayer:

Dear Lord,

I thank You for being the glue that holds me together. Lord, I pray that You remove all anxiousness from me. I choose to pray to You about my problems and trust that You will work things out. Continue to grow me every day that I might be more like You.

In Jesus' name, amen.

How to be Swaggalicious…

1. What things in your life are you anxious about? Why?

2. Do you think God can fix the things you are anxious about? Why or why not?

3. Say a prayer to God about the thing(s) you are

anxious about. Thank Him for where you are and let Him know what you want and need Him to do with those anxious things. If it helps, write your prayer to God below before you pray it out loud.

_____

_____

_____

_____

_____

_____

_____

_____

_____

_____

_____

_____

_____

_____

_____

_____

_____

_____

_____

_____

_____

_____

_____

_____

_____

_____

16.

Makeup

I have always admired women who wear makeup effortlessly. I don't really wear makeup, so I struggle making makeup look so natural. Wearing makeup effortlessly requires skill and ability so that you can enhance the areas you like and cover up the things you don't like.

Makeup is something that, when done right, enhances the beauty of the person wearing it. From eyeshadow, eyeliner, mascara, blush, to lipstick, lip gloss, concealer, and foundation, there are many different types of makeup to hide blemishes, cover up scars, and highlight your best features.

These are the same things Jesus wants to do with His blood. By dying on Calvary, Jesus did away with every blemish in your life and every scar that has been holding you back from being what God has called you to be. While Jesus covers up our blemishes and scars, He also wants to highlight all of our great qualities so that we reflect the person God created us to be.

Isaiah, Chapter 53, verse 5 states that He [Jesus] was "wounded for our transgressions, He was bruised for our iniquities…by His stripes we are healed."This means that **the blood Jesus shed on Calvary covers every sin you have done or will do and brings healing like**

the sin never happened. His blood does the same for every wound that has been inflicted on you by yourself or those around you. Even though makeup can cover up scars and blemishes, it does not have the power to heal. Makeup will always be a temporary fix…a cover-up that has to be put on daily to hide the things we don't want people to see.

Although Jesus' blood covers our sins and scars and wipes them away, we have to believe that our sins and scars truly are healed. Have you ever seen someone whose skin looks amazing? You decide to tell them that their skin is flawless and they respond, "It's my makeup. I have bad acne, but the makeup makes it look like my skin is clear." You might think the person should have just said thank you and not point out the flaws in their skin that you didn't see. However, we do the same with our sin and wounds. When people see you and they compliment all the good things in your life, you inform them of all the things you are struggling with that they don't know about. **Just like you trust that your physical makeup covers your flaws, you have to trust in Jesus' blood wiping your sins away and starting your life anew.** If God doesn't remember our flaws (Psalms 103:12), then we need to wear our "makeup" in confidence knowing we've got concealer and foundation that will never fail!

Scripture: Isaiah 53:5

Affirmation: Jesus' blood covers all my sins and faults and makes me a new creature in Christ

Prayer:

Dear Lord,

Thank You for dying on the cross for me. I thank You that Your blood wipes me clean. Lord, I truly want to walk in the newness You have given me through Your blood. I pray that You increase my confidence in knowing that You have truly made me clean and brand new.

In Jesus' name, amen.

How to be Swaggalicious...

1. What "flaws" do you cover up or try to cover up? Why?

2. Do you believe that Jesus' blood truly heals you from your sin and flaws? Why?

3. What can you do to trust and believe that Jesus's blood has healed you and made you whole?

_____

_____

_____

_____

_____

_____

_____

_____

_____

_____

_____

_____

_____

_____

17.

Confetti

Confetti is small cuts of colored paper normally used at parties or other celebrations for decoration. Confetti comes in all colors and can be put on tables, the floor, or simply thrown in the air. No matter the type of confetti, a few things are always true: (1) you always see confetti at celebrations and (2) confetti gets everywhere and is hard to clean up.

My church was having a Valentine's Day party for the youth, and I volunteered to help decorate. As I was helping decorate the tables with confetti, I realized we didn't have enough for every table. To make sure there was confetti on every table, I had to go around to the tables that were full of confetti and take some confetti off to put on the tables that didn't have confetti. The tables weren't fully covered in confetti, but all of them had some confetti on them as decoration.

Imagine that your Christian life is confetti. How much space would you be able to cover with your confetti? Would you only have enough to decorate one table in a room full of tables or would you be able to cover them all? Would you only cover a small portion of a football stadium or would you be able to cover it all?

Like confetti, **you should be spread everywhere**

and make an impact wherever you are so that people know and remember you were there. After confetti is used at a celebration, small pieces of it continue to stick around so that others know and remember a celebration took place there and confetti was part of the celebration. When you come in contact with people, do you leave them with something good to remember about God?

In Jeremiah, Chapter 20, verse 9, Jeremiah says that he tried to not talk about God, but God's word was like fire in his bones and he couldn't hold back. A fire consumes all that is around it and is hard to put out once it gets started. Jeremiah said that God's word was fire within him which meant that when he spoke God's word, it consumed him and everything around him.

Just like Jeremiah said he couldn't hold back God's word, you should be the same way. Confetti doesn't only impact the area or place that it's used in; it impacts the person who puts it there, too. As you allow God to work in you, His Word will consume you and you won't be able to hold it back so that those around you will be impacted by His Word.

Even if there's only enough confetti for a few tables or only part of a room, it falls over and covers whatever area it's in. That's how your Christian walk should be. Every day when you interact with those around you, you should leave them with some confetti of what God has done and is doing in you. People should have particles/words/expressions from you that get in places that are hard for them to get rid of.

Scripture: Jeremiah 20:9

Affirmation: I am spreading God's word to those around me.

Prayer:

Dear Lord,

I thank You for living on the inside of me. I thank You that you have equipped me to impact the lives of those around me. Lord, I pray that You allow me to increase my impact so that I leave people with a piece of You that will impact their life.

In Jesus' name, amen.

How to be Swaggalicious...

1. What kind of impact do you have on those around you, good or bad?

2. Is this the kind of impact you want to have on others? Why or why not?

3. How can you use your impact to spread God's word?

_____

_____

_____

_____

_____

_____

_____

_____

_____

_____

_____

_____

_____

_____

_____

_____

_____

_____

_____

_____

_____

_____

_____

_____

_____

_____

_____

18.

Cell phone Updates

Cell phone updates are periodic updates that happen to all our phones. These updates improve the function of your phone and fix any issues that might be happening with the phone. In order for updates to take place, your phone has to be shut down and rebooted with the new information so that the phone can function properly.

I am always the last among my family and friends to get the latest phone. My thought is, if my current phone works, why do I need to upgrade my phone? After I see people who have new phones and all that their phone can do, I realize how far behind I am technology wise. With my old cell phone, I wasn't able to get some of the features that the new phones had because they weren't available to my old phone. In the same way, there are some things not available to you because you haven't been updated spiritually. God wants to increase you, but that requires you to be updated.

Picture your Christian life as if it were a cell phone. Do you still have the same mindset and ways that you did when you first got saved? Have you improved or grown in the areas of prayer, knowledge of God, or Bible study? If you're still in the same place that you were in when you first go saved, or ten years ago, five years ago, one year ago; you need an update!

In Matthew, Chapter 9, verse 17, Jesus says that you don't put new wine in old wineskin because the old skin will break and cause the new wine to spill out. Instead, you put new wine in a new wineskin. What this verse is saying is that you can't put new things in old containers. The old wineskin couldn't hold the new because it had become stiff and hard. New wine would expand as it aged, so it could not be put in a hard or stiff wine skin. The wine's growth would cause the skin to break. New wineskins have the ability to stretch and mold around the liquid they contain. God can't put new things in you if you aren't new and renewed. **He can't give you more or take you to a new level with an old mindset or old habits.** You must continually be updated spiritually so that God can pour into you all the things that He wants to give to you.

So while you're updating your cell phone, take the time to determine if you need a spiritual update as well.

Scripture: Matthew 9:17

Affirmation: I am changing and renewing every day so that I can receive all God has for me.

Prayer:

Dear Lord,

I thank You for walking with me every day. I know there are so many blessings You want to pour out on me. I pray that You renew me daily so that I might grow into who You want me to be so that I receive all that You want me to have.

In Jesus' name, amen.

How to be Swaggalicious...

1. What areas do you want to grow in spiritually? Why?

2. What areas have you not grown in spiritually? Why?

3. In what ways can you start growing in these areas?

_____

_____

_____

_____

_____

_____

_____

_____

_____

_____

_____

_____

_____

_____

_____

_____

_____

_____

_____

_____

_____

19.

Flowers

Flowers are beautiful and colorful and brighten up any area they are placed in. They come in an array of colors and can grow almost anywhere. No matter what type of flowers you like, they all require work to be put into them for them to thrive and grow.

As long as I can remember, my mom has always planted flowers on the outside of our house. As soon as the weather grew warm, she purchased annuals to plant. While the flowers always looked good in the store, she had to work with them when she got them home for them to stay that way. She had to water and fertilize the flowers, and tend to their soil.

The same is true in your Christian life. When you're in a church service surrounded by other Christians, you feel good about the Word that you heard and you're excited about what God will do in your life. After you leave the service, you have to do work to make sure that the Word you heard is able to produce a harvest in your life. If you leave church and don't water or feed the Word you received, the Word won't take root within you and you will not be able to grow.

In Mark, Chapter 4, Jesus tells a story about a farmer planting seeds. There was seed that didn't make it to the soil because it was eaten, and seed that fell on rocky soil and dried up with the sun. There were other seeds that fell among weeds and died because the weeds took over. Finally, there were a group of seeds that fell on good ground and were able to grow and multiply because they developed roots. This story shows that all of us may hear the same Word of God, but it develops in all of us differently depending on what happens to the Word.

Just like flowers need water and sunlight to grow, you need to study the Bible, pray, and learn more about God to grow in your walk and relationship with Him. **Without growth, you will wither and die just like a flower that hasn't gotten any water.** Prayer and the Bible are the nutrients we need as Christians to grow into what God is calling us to be.

When you see flowers, think about what had to happen for them to be the vibrant and colorful flowers you see. Remember that you are God's flower and for you to be vibrant and colorful, you have to allow the nutrients of God to feed you so that you can bloom into the flower God wants you to be.

Scripture: Mark 4

Affirmation: I am rooted in God and growing into who He wants me to be.

Prayer:

Dear Lord,

Thank You for Your Word. I pray that Your Word grows and develops in me that I might grow deeper in You so that I can become who you want me to be. I pray that

You remove all things that would try to hinder Your Word from taking root in my life.

In Jesus' name, amen.

How to be Swaggalicious...

1. Are you letting God's Word take root in your life? Why or why not?

2. What areas in your life do you need God to brighten or bring growth?

3. List things that you can do to make sure God's Word develops roots and brings growth.

_____

_____

_____

_____

_____

_____

_____

_____

_____

_____

_____

_____

_____

_____

_____

_____

_____

_____

_____
_____
_____
_____
_____
_____
_____
_____
_____
_____
_____
_____
_____
_____
_____
_____
_____
_____
_____

20.

Shades

Shades are a fashion accessory that also serve the purpose of protection. Protection happens when something is a barrier between you and anything that could be harmful to you. Airbags in your car protect you from getting hurt if you're in a car accident. Sunglasses and hats protect you from sun rays when you go outside. No matter what you use for protection, the purpose is always to keep you safe from something that may hurt you.

We should view God's presence in our life like shades. When you accepted Christ as your Savior, His presence surrounded and covered you. **Just like wearing shades gives protection from the sun, wearing God gives you protection from all things that the Devil will bring your way.**

While these shades provide protection, you may still be impacted by the trials you have to go through. Having God's presence in your life will protect you, but you will still have to go through difficult things in your life. The beauty of His protection is that He covers you through all things so that the impact isn't as bad as it would've been if He weren't there.

Psalms 91 talks about the safety that we have when we abide in God's presence. Verse 2 says He is a refuge and a fortress. A refuge is a place that you go to for shelter and protection and a fortress is a place protected from attack. This means that having God's presence in your life means you have a place to go for protection and when you get to His place, you are protected from any attacks you may face.

Having God's presence surround you doesn't mean He stifles you so that you can't do anything or He gives you so much freedom that you don't know He's there. Having God's presence with you means you have relationship with Him. He knows about you and you know about Him. Because you know about each other, He knows when you need help and you know when you need to go to Him for shelter and protection.

Having God's presence with you means that when you step out, people see how He is all over you. They may not know what it is, but they know something is different about you because you look different, walk different, and are just different all around. So as you put on those shades before you go out, take time to evaluate if God's presence is what you put on to stay protected from all the harm that may come your way.

Scripture: Psalms 91

Affirmation: I run to God for shelter and safety.

Prayer:

Dear Lord,

I thank You for watching over me and protecting me. I pray that Your presence cover me daily and protect me from dangers seen and unseen. I pray that You overshadow me so much that people see You reflected through me.

In Jesus' name, amen.

How to be Swaggalicious…

1. Where do you go when you want to feel safe? Why?

2. Read Psalm 91. What does it say God protects you from?

3. What things in your life can you look to God for protection from?

_____

_____

_____

_____

_____

_____

_____

_____

_____

_____

_____

_____

_____

_____

_____

_____

_____

_____

_____

21.

Eyeglasses

Traditionally, glasses are accessories that you put on your face to help you see. Some people only need them for reading while others need them to do everything. More recently, eyewear is considered to be a fashion statement so people who don't even need corrective lenses are wearing it.

You may be one of the lucky few that don't need glasses to read or to see in front of you. I need glasses for all that and more. I have been wearing glasses since I was eight years old. Without my glasses, everything around me is fuzzy and hard to make out. But with my glasses, my vision is almost perfect! I can see like everyone else who is not wearing glasses. I don't need someone to read a sign for me or point out something in the distance because I have my glasses and can see things clearly for myself.

Having the Holy Spirit is like me and my glasses. When you have the Holy Spirit with you, His presence enables you to see clearer. **Walking with the Holy Spirit allows you to see what's coming toward you and what you're headed to.** Being able to see clearer with the Holy Spirit, means you can avoid stumbling blocks and tripping over things you wouldn't see without Him being there. When you don't have the Holy

Spirit, you're like me without my glasses. Everything is fuzzy; you don't know what's around you or where you're going.

Imagine having to filter your walk with God through your mom's or friend's experiences or eyes. Your relationship with God would depend on them getting the Word and them getting the Spirit. But like my glasses, if you really want to see clearer, you have to put on the glasses for yourself! The Holy Spirit may move in your friend's life, your mother's life, or your sister's life, but He only moves in your life when you decide to put Him on and seek Him for guidance to make your vision clearer.

In John chapter 14, verse 26, Jesus tells the disciples that God will send them a Helper, the Holy Spirit, and that the Holy Spirit would teach them all things. This means that the Holy Spirit gives us guidance, wisdom, and understanding for everything that we go to Him about. Are you not sure about a big test that you have coming up? Pray and ask the Holy Spirit to show you what you need to study and focus on, and He will teach you what you need to know.

When I was working on my doctorate, I had to take an exam that would determine if I stayed in the program and moved forward to earn my doctorate. The exam was eight hours and over two days and very intense. I knew I needed help studying for this exam, so before I studied, I asked the Holy Spirit to show me what I needed to focus on while I was studying. When I went in to take my exam and started looking at the exam questions, I wanted to scream and do a church run. Every question on the exam was what the Holy

Spirit showed me when I was studying. I still had to do my part in preparing for the exam, but when I asked the Holy Spirit for guidance, he showed me what to do and helped me see clearer where things were fuzzy.

My story may not seem real to you, but it was very real to me. I challenge you that if you have areas in your life where you want direction, clarity, wisdom, or knowledge…ask the Holy Spirit to show to you those things. God sent Him to be our Teacher, but He can't teach if we don't ask questions and sit down so He can give us instruction.

Scripture: John 14:26

Affirmation: The Holy Spirit gives me guidance and direction.

Prayer:

Dear Lord,

Thank You for sending the Holy Spirit to give guidance, instruction, and direction. Holy Spirit I pray that You show me [INSERT WHAT YOU WANT THE HOLY SPIRIT TO SHOW]. I thank You for Your guidance and will trust in what You say.

In Jesus' name, amen.

How to be Swaggalicious…

1. What areas in your life do you want more clarity and direction on (purpose, school, career path)?

2. What have you done to try and get clarity and

direction in that area (s)?

3. Pray and ask the Holy Spirit to give you clarity and direction on the areas that you mentioned in number 1. So that you can have a record of what you prayed about, use the space below to write your prayer.

_____

_____

_____

_____

_____

_____

_____

_____

_____

_____

_____

_____

_____

_____

_____

_____

_____

_____

_____

_____

_____

_____

_____

_____

_____

_____

_____

22.

Chargers

Power is having control, authority, or influence over something or someone. While we all have some form of power, we all have different levels of power. No matter what level of power you have, all power comes from a source or being connected to something or someone.

Imagine your cell phone when you first get it. You're only able to use it after you connect it to a power source and it gets charged. Although it will go a while without being connected to its power, the battery will eventually die and you'll have to reconnect it to a power source again. You can't connect it to any power source for it to get recharged. You have to connect it to the right power source. If your car battery dies and you need to recharge it, connecting your cell phone charger to the battery won't get the car started. Only a battery specifically made for an automobile will recharge the car and get it moving.

Like your phone and automobile, if you lose power, you have to connect to the right source to keep moving forward. You may look to money, relationships, a job, or partying for your power but looking to these is like using a cellphone charger to recharge a car battery. They just won't work. After Jesus rose from the grave,

He told the disciples that all authority (power) had been given to Him in heaven and on earth (Matthew 28:18). If Jesus has all power, that means He is a power source. As a follower of Christ, He is our power source. But just like your phone is only charged when it is plugged in, **you have to be connected to Jesus to get His power**.

As a Christian, there are two ways to connect to your God power source for a recharge. The first way is through prayer. James 5:16 says,"the earnest prayer of a righteous person has great power and produces wonderful results."(NLT) When we pray heartfelt and honest prayers, our spirits are renewed and energized because we know God hears our prayers and is moving in our situation on our behalf.

The second way to connect is through fasting. In Daniel, chapter 1, the Scripture says Daniel refused to eat the meat and wine of the king. He and his men only ate vegetables. At the end of their fast, they had more strength than those who ate the meat and drank the wine. And from this, God enabled Daniel to interpret the king's dreams.

A fast is when you deny yourself food for a period of time while you pray to God seeking knowledge, wisdom, and insight. If you have ever done a spiritual fast, do you notice that you have more energy and strength when you're going through a fast? While it may seem like fasting will cause you to be weak physically, fasting strengthens you to be able to do more because you're denying things that you want -- certain foods or drinks -- and trusting and depending on God to sustain you which strengthens you spiritually.

So the next time your power goes out and you

need to reconnect to the source, remember prayer and fasting are the plugs that will get you there.

Scripture: Ephesians 6:10

Affirmation: All my power comes from God.

Prayer:

Dear Lord,

Thank You for being my source. I thank You that I can come to You when I am weak and need to be energized. I pray that You help me embrace the power that You have given me so that I can do what You have called me to do.

In Jesus' name, amen.

How to be Swaggalicious...

If you want more information on fasting, please see the Appendix.

1. What do you do when you need to reenergize yourself?

2. How do these things help reenergize you?

3. Read Daniel 1:1-17. What foods did Daniel eat on his fast and how long was his fast? What does it say God gave him after his fast?

_____

_____

_____

_____

23.

Tracker

Trackers are new technologies that monitor your steps and fitness activity. More advanced trackers monitor your heart rate and sleeping patterns. Regardless of the type of tracker you have, they all keep a record of what you do on a daily basis.

In an effort to increase my daily physical activity, I decided to purchase a fitness tracker to count my steps, calories, and exercise. At the end of every day, the tracker shows me how many steps I've gotten, how many calories I've burned, and how many minutes of exercise I have gotten. Before I purchased this tracker, I always assumed I was getting a lot of steps, burning a lot of calories, and getting many minutes of exercise, but I wasn't. With the tracker, there was a record of all that I had done for the day in black and white and there was no denying the stats in front of me, good or bad.

Imagine my fitness tracker being a spiritual tracker keeping a tally on all the spiritual things I do every day. If you had one, how would it say you spend your day? Would it show that you pray and read your Bible every day, speak kind words to those you encounter, and help those around you when you can? Without a spiritual tracker, we can choose to believe we are doing spiritual things on a daily basis because no one sees what we do and there is no record. We can deceive ourselves and others.

In the same way our fitness tracker details what we've done so we can make adjustments to improve our stats for the next day, our spiritual tracker can do the same. We may say we don't have a "spiritual" tracker, but we do. The Holy Spirit helps us live this Christian life so that we reflect God and become who He called us to be. The Holy Spirit will nudge us to say "hi" to someone or tell us to not go to the party. **The Holy Spirit is the tracker that helps us grade ourselves daily on our spiritual walk.** Even though we will have days where our stats may not be the best (no prayer, no Bible study, mean to friends or family), God always gives us the opportunity to improve our stats. Like my fitness tracker, each day, my stats start all over again. So if I had a bad day yesterday, I can choose to make today a great day by doing more than I did the day before.

In Romans Chapter 7, verses 15-20, Paul talks about the battle he faces daily with his flesh. Essentially, Paul says that the things he wants to do (pray, read his Bible) he doesn't do. Instead, he does the things that he doesn't want to do. Does this mean that Paul isn't right with God or is a failure? It doesn't. Paul goes on to say that the sin in him is what makes him do the things that he doesn't want to do. Paul is not giving an excuse for sin. Paul is reminding us that every day is a struggle to do the right thing because your flesh wants to do things opposite of what your spirit wants to do. Because we were born into sin (Psalm 51:5), we battle our flesh on a daily basis.

Remember, that this Christian walk will have ups

and downs. If you use your "spiritual" tracker to keep a tally on your daily walk, you will always be able to improve your walk day to day so that you can become the woman God created you to be.

Scripture: Romans 7:15-20

Affirmation: I am growing in God daily.

Prayer:

Dear Lord,

I thank You for where You have brought me from. I thank You for where you are taking me to. I pray that You grow my spirit daily and suppress the desires of my flesh that do not line up with Your Word and Your will for my life.

In Jesus' name, amen.

How to be Swaggalicious…

1. What spiritual things would you like to do on a daily basis (pray, read your Bible, meditate)?

2. What is stopping you from doing the things you listed in question number 1?

3. Decide which of the things in number 1 you want to start doing first. After you have decided that, plan a daily time for you to do this thing and put it in your phone so that you have a reminder. Make sure to schedule it at a time when you will have at least fifteen to thirty minutes of uninterrupted time. This may be in the morning before going to work, during a break at

work, or right before you go to bed. The time doesn't matter; being consistent does. Doing spiritual things daily is no different than anything else that you do. You need to make it a habit for you to stick with it. To help you keep track of what you're doing, you can list the thing you want to start doing daily below and the day and time you're going to do it.

_____

_____

_____

_____

_____

_____

_____

_____

_____

_____

_____

_____

_____

_____

_____

_____

_____

_____

_____

_____

_____

_____

_____

_____

_____

_____

24.

Cake

Who doesn't like cake? It's soft, sweet, and covered in creamy frosting. I must admit, I have always liked cake. Recently, I have started liking the extravagantly decorated cakes. I think it's amazing what skilled bakers can do to transform regular cake into something that doesn't even look like a bakery item. Since I've started baking, I have always wanted my cakes to look like the ones I see on television and in magazines. But that requires a lot of time, training, and I'm sure skill to get the results I want.

The Christian walk is similar to the beautiful cakes that I admire. When a person first gets saved, they want to look and be like the Christians they see being all God has called them to be and being truly blessed. What we don't see is that just like a beautiful cake, they didn't start out that way. After God mixes up things in our lives, like the process for baking a cake, He puts us through the fire, like an oven. After going through the fire, we come out ready, like a plain cake -- done on the inside but not looking the way God wants us to look.

In Jeremiah Chapter 18, verse 6, the prophet delivers a message from the Lord where-in the Lord tells the people that He is the potter and they are the clay. This means that God takes us through different twists and turns to mold us into who He wants us to be. This requires God to trim off some things that we don't need like friends, relationships, mindsets, and attitudes so that He can build us into the beautiful cake that He wants and a cake others will enjoy. Once God is finished trimming us, He starts putting us back together by adding all the sweet things people like (grace and mercy). Not only do these sweet things add value to us (who wants a cake without icing?), they help keep us together. Just like cake layers won't stay together without frosting, we wouldn't stay together without God's grace, mercy, and blessings -- the sweet things in life (James 4:6).

After God adds the sweet things to us, He just keeps adding them as we continue to go through the process of having Him make us into a beautiful cake that is fully decorated with sprinkles, bows, beads, colors, or any other decorative item that shows off the beauty of the cake and the skills of the baker (Matthew 5:16). While this process is long, **God never gets tired or frustrated with us. Since He is the Baker, He knows how to change things so that He can get the product He desires.**

So the next time you're eating a slice of cake, remember that just like the cake had to go through a process to get to its end result, you must go through a process, too. This process won't be easy, but remember that God, the Baker, knows your potential and knows the ingredients you're made out of. He knows your ending and will do all that He can to fashion you into the beautiful cake He made you to be.

Scripture: Jeremiah 18:6

Affirmation: God is molding me into something great.

Prayer:

Dear Lord,

I thank You for what You have brought me through. I thank You for the trials and twists in my life that have developed me into the person I am today. I pray that You continue to mold and shape me so that others can see Your great work in me and glorify You.

In Jesus' name, amen.

How to be Swaggalicious...

1. What in your life do you think needs to be cut out (friends, old boyfriends, bad attitude)? Why?

2. Have you tried to cut any of these things out of your life in the past? What happened?

3. What will you do today to remove these things from your life?

_____

_____

_____

_____

_____

_____

_____

_____

_____

_____

_____

_____

_____

_____

_____

_____

_____

_____

_____

_____

_____

_____

_____

_____

_____

_____

_____

_____

_____

25.

Alarm

Alarms are devices that alert you to possible danger, to get ready for something, or to something coming up like a birthday party or appointment. When I was in college, I used to always look forward to Saturday because that would be my morning to sleep in. But like clockwork, I arose the same time on Saturday mornings as I did during the week. It was pretty frustrating because I wanted to rest, but my body was used to being up at a certain time. I awoke without setting an alarm.

Just like my body naturally got up without an alarm on a Saturday, our body should naturally do the things God wants us to do. We should be able to do the things He needs us to do because we have practiced the habit of consistency. Christian lifestyle activities should be a part of who we are.

When I was in college, I decided to get serious about my prayer life. I would wake up really early in the morning to pray and read my Bible. It became such a part of my routine that I still do it today. I changed the time I pray from early morning to late morning, but my body always wakes up for prayer even if I don't set an alarm because I have been doing it consistently for years.

If you want to grow in your Christian walk, you have to set "alarms" to remind you to do spiritual things. Just like your body doesn't want to get up in the morning, your body doesn't want to pray, read the Bible, go to church, or go to Bible study. You have to treat your "alarms" for spiritual things like you treat alarms for worldly things. If you don't set an alarm for work, you may be late and face consequences with your boss. If you don't set an "alarm" to pray, you will not develop a strong relationship with God and will have to deal with problems that may have not been an issue had you gotten up to pray (James 5:16).

Many times you may not feel like going to school or work, but you still go. You need to treat the things of God the same way. **Behavior only becomes part of your life when you do it on a regular basis.** 1 Samuel Chapter 15, verse 22 says that obedience is better than sacrifice. This means that if God told us to pray, we need to pray because we should want to be obedient to His Word.

So the next time you hit the snooze button on the alarm, make sure you aren't hitting snooze on your spiritual "alarm" so that you can make the things of God a natural part of your life.

Scripture: 1 Samuel 15:22

Affirmation: I am obedient to what God wants me to do.

Prayer:

Dear Lord,

Thank You for wanting the best for me despite my shortcomings and my faults. I pray that You change my desires to reflect Yours so that the things of You become second nature to me and become part of my daily routine.

In Jesus' name, amen.

How to be Swaggalicious…

1. Think about your daily schedule. When do you have free time?

2. What do you do during your free time?

3. Will you commit to spending some of your free time to doing things that will grow you spiritually in God? If so, what will you commit to do and how often? To keep you accountable, list them below.

_____

_____

_____

_____

_____

_____

_____

_____

_____

_____

_____

_____

_____

_____

_____

_____

_____

_____

_____

_____

_____

_____

_____

_____

_____

_____

_____

_____

_____

_____

_____

_____

_____

_____

_____

26.

Open Back

I have always liked dresses that have an open back. Something that shows just enough, but never fully exposes anything. Growing up, my mom always told my sister and me that we couldn't have everything hanging out. If we were going to wear something short that showed our legs, then everything else needed to be covered up. If we were going to wear a top with a deep v in the front, then everything else needed to be covered up. If we were going to wear something that had an open back, then our chest had to be covered up. She wanted to make sure that we weren't exposing all parts of ourselves when we went out.

God is the same way with our heart as my mom was with our clothes. God doesn't want us fully exposing our heart to everyone as we move throughout our day-to-day life. Proverbs Chapter 4, verse 23 says that we should guard our heart because the issues of life come from our heart. This means that what is inside of us is displayed in what we do, so we should guard ourselves from things that would cause us to do things or display things that are not pleasing to God. Proverbs 23:7 says that as a man thinks in his heart, so is he. This means that whatever you think in your heart shows who you really are. For something to get in your heart, you have to open yourself up to it. Does this mean that you never expose your heart? It doesn't. **While God wants you to guard your heart, He doesn't want you to be closed off from the world and never open yourself up to friendships, family, and other relationships. He just wants you to be smart about the people you open yourself up to.** Living a fully guarded life will leave you empty because you will never have the experience of friendship and closeness with those around you. You have to make the choice to let God and the Holy Spirit guide you and give you discernment to know when to expose your heart and to whom.

Think about your heart like an open back dress. When a woman walks into a room with an open back dress, people in the room don't know who she is. From the front, she is covered and guarded, so they aren't sure of her attitude or if she is approachable. As she moves through the room, they notice that her back is open. While they still aren't sure of who she is, they start to see the parts of herself that she shares with them and have a better picture of who she is.

So the next time you find yourself afraid of opening up to people for them to see who you truly are, remember that your heart is like an open back dress. You don't expose everything when you first meet people, but you reveal what you want to share so they can see parts of you to get a better picture of you and the person God made you to be.

Scripture: Proverbs 4:23

Affirmation: I am open to sharing myself with those

around me.

Prayer:

Dear Lord,

I thank You for being in my life. I pray that You help me guard my heart at the same that that You help me let my guard down. I pray for wisdom and discernment to know when my guard should be up and when I need to let it down.

In Jesus' name, amen.

How to be Swaggalicious…

1. What do you do when you meet new people?

2. Do you think you give too much of yourself too soon to those around you? Why or why not?

3. What steps can you take to make sure that you guard your heart?

_____

_____

_____

_____

_____

_____

_____

_____

_____

_____

_____

27.

Long hair, Don't care

Even if you don't have long hair, please read on. This will still apply to you.

In today's society, many have become obsessed with long hair. It seems that no one wants to have short hair or wear their own hair because they want long, flowing hair. I have been fortunate that my hair usually grows rather fast and for most of my life has been long. But right before I turned twenty-two, I wanted a change and decided to cut almost all of my hair off. I went from hair past my shoulders to chin length hair. While I liked my new look, everyone around me thought I was going crazy and was having identity issues. They could not understand why I cut off all my hair. What they couldn't understand was that I was growing into me and part of that growth involved me cutting my hair. I wanted change.

Just like I decided to cut my hair because I was looking for a change, your Christian walk will take you through many changes. 1 Corinthians, Chapter 13 verse 11 says that when I was a child, I spoke as a child but when I became a man, I put away childish things. When you first start your walk with God, you will do things that a child does. As a baby Christian, you may struggle with forgiveness, praying for your enemies, or doing things that glorify God. As you mature and grow in the things of God, you will move from a child to a teenager to a young adult to an adult. As you become a mature Christian, you shouldn't have a problem forgiving those who do bad thing things to you, praying for your enemies, and displaying behavior that glorifies God.

Cutting my hair was a decision that wouldn't change my life drastically. I decided to do it regardless of others' thoughts. That's the way you have to be when you step out into what God is telling you to do or calling you to do. Hebrews 11:1 says that faith is the substance of things hoped for, the evidence of things not seen. This means that **this walk with God will cause you to step out into things that you don't see which will cause people around you to think you're crazy**. You may even think you're crazy because what you're doing doesn't make sense. But if you know that you're doing what's right, then you don't need to worry about what others, including your family, have to say. Just like you're focused on what God is telling you to do, you need to trust that He will work on them and that they will eventually come around. Even if they don't, you're still in a good spot because you listened to God.

So the next time you're feeling unsure in the decisions you're making that are good for you, remember that God is with you so you should be confident in who He made you to be and what He has given you.

Scripture: 1 Corinthians 13:11

Affirmation: I am confident in where God is taking me and the road He has me on.

Prayer:

Dear Lord,

Thank You for bringing me this far. I thank You for my growth, and I am excited about where You are taking me. I pray that You keep me confident in Your will for my life and that I stay focused on You and what You would have me to do.

In Jesus' name, amen.

How to be Swaggalicious...

1. What habits do you think you display that don't glorify God? Why?

2. What things of God would you like to grow in? Why?

3. What childish things do you need to put away, now that you are becoming a woman? Why?

_____

_____

_____

_____

_____

_____

_____

_____

_____

_____

_____

_____

28.

Rain

In the city where I live, we experience rain showers without warning and at a moment's notice, so you have to always be prepared for a potential rain shower or storm. For that reason, I always carry an umbrella with me. So I never get soaked if I'm caught in unpredictable weather.

Just like I try to always be prepared for a physical rainstorm, as Christians we have to always be prepared for a spiritual "rainstorm" or trials that come. While we may not like trials, we know they are coming, so why would we not prepare for them? In Matthew, Chapter 5 verse 45 it says that God makes the sun rise on the evil and the good and sends rain on the just and the unjust. Since we know that rain or hard times come to those who are followers of Christ, we shouldn't be surprised when it happens. Imagine a teacher who hasn't prepared lessons for the classes they have to teach. We would think, why didn't they prepare when they knew the first day of school was coming?

Just like a teacher not being prepared for their classes doesn't make sense, a Christian not being prepared for a spiritual "rainstorm" doesn't make sense either. To prepare for spiritual "rainstorms" you have to be in prayer on a consistent basis and be in God's Word consistently. Prayer and His Word are the umbrella and rain jacket that keep you dry while a "rainstorm" is breaking out around you.

While rain brings storms, it also brings life. After it rains, flowers bloom and are brighter and grass begins to grow and becomes greener. **Things are always better after the rain because the rain comes to bring life and wash away things that don't need to be there.** Psalm 30:5 says that weeping endures for a night, but joy comes in the morning. Even though you will endure rain, know that when the "rain" is over, you will come out brighter and stronger and rejoicing!!

So remember to be prepared for the rain that is coming by having your umbrella and rain jacket so that you can stay dry and come out bright and strong on the other side!

Scripture: Matthew 5:45

Affirmation: I embrace God's rain in my life.

Prayer:

Dear Lord,

Thank You for your rain. I know that Your rain comes to make me stronger and that I will rejoice when the sun comes out. I pray that You keep me strong as I go through the rain so that You can be glorified through me.

In Jesus' name, amen.

How to be Swaggalicious...

1. What trials have you faced in your life?

2. Were you prepared for these trails? How did you deal with these trials?

3. How can you handle trials better in the future?

_____

_____

_____

_____

_____

_____

_____

_____

_____

_____

_____

_____

_____

_____

_____

_____

_____

_____

_____

_____

_____

_____

29.

Earrings

Whether, studs or clip-ons, earrings are always worn as a pair. If something happens to this pair -- one goes missing or one is broken, the earrings are usually thrown out. I used to have a pair of rectangular, glass earrings that I wore with everything. After wearing them for a year or two, I broke one earring beyond repair. Webster's Dictionary defines broken as being separated into parts by being hit or damaged or not working properly. While one earring wasn't broken, the broken earring made both earrings unusable. I ended up throwing those earrings away because they couldn't be worn as a pair anymore so they couldn't be used.

Sometimes you may go through things in life that make you feel broken or leave you broken in self-esteem, spirit, confidence, or ambition. When you feel broken, you walk around in pieces and everyone can see the different parts of you. You may be able to still function, but like my earrings, you don't have the same look or the same life that you had before you became broken.

When we break a plate or a glass, we normally throw it away because we don't want to take the time to fix it or put it back together. When you are broken, you can't just throw yourself away. Although you may not be willing to take the time to fix a broken earring, **God is always willing to take all of your broken pieces and put you back together**.

Psalm 34:18 says that the Lord is close to the brokenhearted and saves those crushed in spirit. This means God is with you when you feel broken and crushed and think that you can't go on. God knows you will face trials and tribulations and daily life that may break down the things He built in you (ambition, confidence, fight, spirit). Because He made you and knows all the potential He put in you, He doesn't want you to stay broken. He is willing to put you back together so that you look as good as you did when He first created you!

Even though God is willing to fix you, you have to be willing to give Him your broken pieces. There may be projects around your house that you might try to fix yourself, but there are some items that you have to take to the manufacturer or call in a professional. Your broken pieces are things that you can't fix by yourself. Jesus says in Matthew, Chapter 11 verse 28-30 for all who are weary and burdened to come to Him and He will give them rest. He says that you will find rest for your soul. But the key to having this rest is to come to Him. You need your manufacturer (God) to fix your broken pieces.

The next time you feel a part of you is broken, don't try to fix it yourself or turn to others for help. They didn't manufacture you. To be restored to your original self, you need to go to your God manufacturer and let Him fix your broken pieces.

Scripture: Matthew 11:28-30

Affirmation: I am giving my burdens to God.

Prayer:

Dear Lord,

I thank You for loving me past my broken pieces. I pray that You give me the strength to surrender my burdens and broken pieces to You so that You can give me rest and put me back together again.

In Jesus' name, amen.

How to be Swaggalicious...

1. In what areas do you feel you are broken? Why?

2. How long have you felt broken?

3. Are you willing to give your burdens to God and let him fix your broken pieces? Why or why not? If you said yes, what are you going to do today to give your burdens to God?

_____

_____

_____

_____

_____

_____

_____

_____

_____

_____

30.

Love

This last devotional is not like the ones before. We have looked at clothes, jewelry, bags, and shoes. But this devotional talks about something that can't be compared to any physical item. This item is the ultimate accessory that every Swaggalicious woman should have because without love, nothing else matters.

Love is one of those feelings and emotions that people find hard to describe. Some say days seem better, life seems brighter, and they feel they can face anything in the world because they have the love and support of someone who cares. Whether romantic, family, or platonic, love is something that we all need and desire. **Love is that thing that allows you to see yourself through the eyes of someone else and should make you want to be your best self.**

This is how God wants us to feel about His love for us. He wants us to have that pep in our step, to see things in a brighter way, and to know we can face anything because His love surrounds us. Most importantly, God wants us to see ourselves the way He see us—overcomer, healthy, ambitious, smart, beautiful. If we wake up every day and see ourselves the way God sees us, we will be able to do above and beyond our dreams.

While romantic, family, or platonic love requires us to do something before we receive it, God's love comes without conditions. John Chapter 3, verse 16 says that God loved the world so He gave His only Son that those who believe in Him will not perish but have everlasting life. This Scripture says God loved the world, so He gave. It doesn't say He loved only the people in the world who loved Him or the people who spoke nice about Him; it says He loved the world. That means God loves everyone and gave His Son to die for everyone, those who will believe in Him and those who will not. This Scripture shows that we did nothing to earn God's love, neither is there anything we can do to lose it or to make Him take it away or make Him love us less. Because His love is unconditional, He takes us as we are, flaws and all.

If you're like me and didn't have the love of one or both parents growing up, this kind of love may seem unreal. You may not be able to fathom someone showing you unmerited and unconditional love. Remember that God is not like man (Numbers 23:19) so His love is not like man's love. God will never hurt you or leave you.

When you feel you can't make it through, know God's love will help push you to see every trial or obstacle to the end. When you feel you're not worthy and are lacking, remember God sees you as worthy and whole. When you feel like no one accepts you for who you are, remember **God made you and loves you just the way you are!**

Scripture: John 3:16

Affirmation: God's love surrounds me every day.

Prayer:

Dear Lord,

Thank You for loving me just the way I am. Because of Your love, I am able to love myself and those around me. I pray that I continue to embrace Your love for me so that I am pushed to be all that You have called me to be.

In Jesus' name, amen.

How to be Swaggalicious...

1. Have you experienced love? What did you have to do to receive this love?

2. Do you feel you are worthy of God's love? Why or why not?

3. Do you think God should put conditions on the love He has for us? Why or why not?

_____

_____

_____

_____

_____

_____

_____

_____

_____

_____

_____

_____

Appendix

Fasting

If you have never been on a fast but would like to try it, here are some things to keep in mind.

1. Decide what you are fasting for (job, test, healing for parent)

2. Find Scriptures that support what you are praying and asking for during your fast

3. Decide what food or drink you are giving up. It doesn't matter what you give up, it matters that you stay consistent. If you have dietary restrictions or your body is feeling weak, then add what you need to your diet so that you are healthy.

4. Decide how long you're going to do your fast. If you are just starting, I recommend that you do it for one day and see how your body handles it. It doesn't matter how long your fast is, it matters that you are consistent with what you say and that you are praying to God while you're fasting.

If you have more questions about fasting, the following book is a good resource:

Fasting: Opening the Door to a Deeper, More Intimate, More Powerful Relationship with God

by Jentezen Franklin

Praying

If you want to grow in your prayer life, but aren't sure how, here are some steps to help you get started.

1. Realize that prayer is simply having conversation with God. Think of prayer with God like talking to your best friend. You should be open, honest, and allow Him to speak to you while you're praying.

2. If you're not sure how to pray, write down your prayers and then say them out loud.

3. Start prayer by thanking God for all that He has done for you. If you don't like it when people only talk to you when they want something, how do you think God feels if we just ask Him for things without thanking Him for what He has already given?

4. Pray for others (family, friends, enemies) first and any needs they may have.

5. Find Scriptures to support what you are praying for. Having Scriptures allows you to remind God what He said He would do about your situation in His word.

6. Pray for the things you need God to do for you.

7. Once you ask God for something in prayer, He heard you. You don't have to continue praying the same thing. Begin thanking Him for the prayer being answered.

If you want more insight on prayer, the following book

is a good resource:

Fervent: A Woman's Battle Plan for Serious, Specific, and Strategic Prayer

by Priscilla Shirer

About the Author

Krista Mincey has a passion to help young women and men embrace all that God created them to be so they can reach their full potential. She was born and raised a proud southern girl from Georgia who now resides in New Orleans, Louisiana where she is works as a professor at Xavier University of Louisiana. She received her bachelor's degree from Georgia College & State University, her masters from Armstrong State University, and her doctorate from Georgia Southern University. She is a member of Greater St. Stephen Full Gospel Baptist Church where she serves as the Director of the Young Adult Ministry. She is a mentor, advisor, friend, daughter, and sister. Every day she prays that she impacts those around her in a positive way by allowing God's light to shine through her. In her day job, she is an assistant professor teaching students about their health and the world around them. In her spare time, she enjoys baking.

Website – www.kristamincey.com

Social Media –

Twitter @dockdblue

Instagram-@kristamincey

Facebook- fans of Krista Mincey

Made in the USA
Columbia, SC
25 November 2017